talkabout
the park

Talk about the playground

The use of too many questions has been avoided, as it is more important to encourage comment and discussion than to expect particular answers.

Care has been taken to retain sufficient realism in the illustrations and subject matter to enable a young child to have fun identifying objects, creatures and situations.

It is wise to remember that patience and understanding are very important, and that children do not all develop evenly or at the same rate. Parents should not be anxious if children do not give correct answers to those questions that are asked. With help, they will do so in their own time.

The brief notes at the back of this book will enable interested parents to make the fullest use of these **Ladybird talkabout** books.

Ladybird Books Loughborough

compiled by Ethel Wingfield

illustrated by Eric Winter, Harry Wingfield and Martin Aitchison

The publishers wish to acknowledge the assistance of the nursery school advisers who helped with the preparation of this book,
especially that of Lady Britton, Chairman,
and Miss M Puddephat, M Ed, Vice Chairman
of The British Association for Early Childhood Education (formerly The Nursery School Association).

Talk about the picture

Have you seen these?

Talk about the colours

Tell the story

WET
PAINT

3

4

Talk about
the picture

Match the pictures
with the
black shapes

Have you heard these?

Talk about 'big' and 'little', 'large and 'small'

M.A.

Who owns
which dog?

Talk about Spring

Talk about summer

Talk about autumn

Talk about winter

LOOK
and find
another
like this
and this
and this

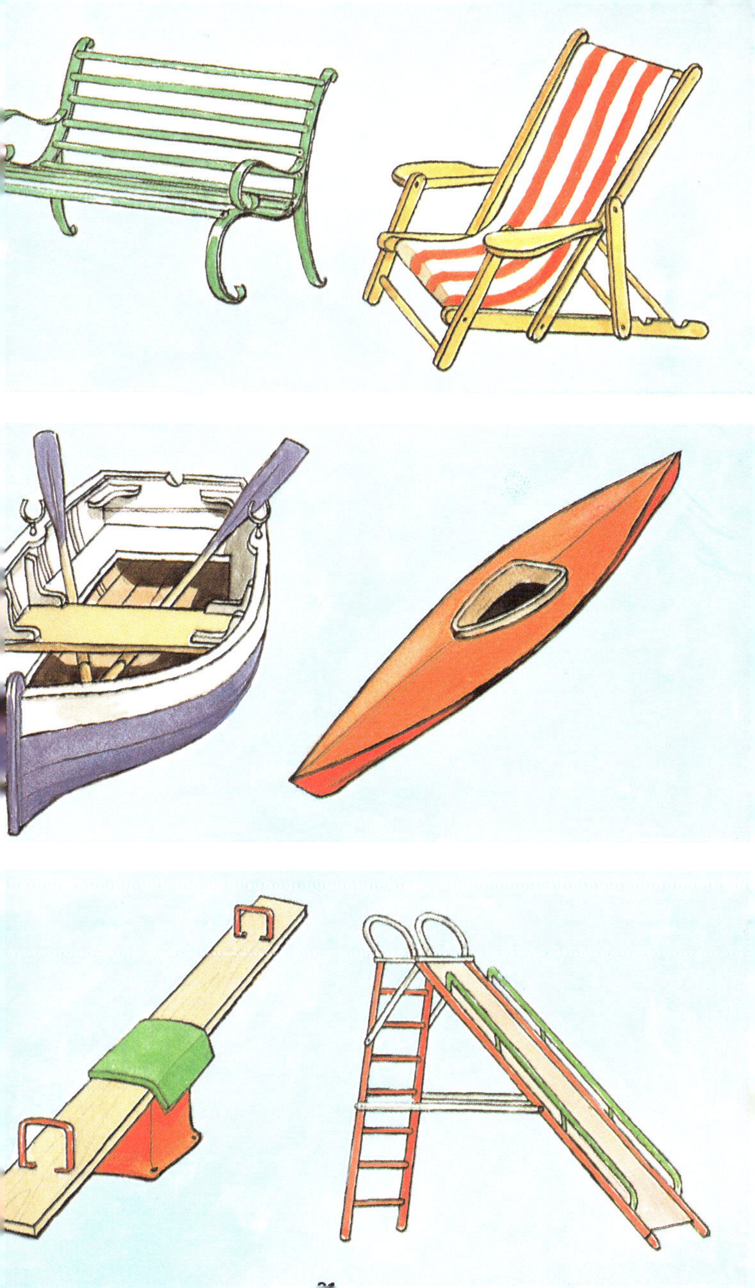

Tell the story

1

2

3

4

Talk about
the colours

What are the children doing?

1
2
3
4
5

1
2
3
ow many
ucklings?
ow many
ucklings?

Talk about what the men are doing

What is everyone doing?

Which should we put in the basket?

How many childre
are on the slide?

How many are on
the roundabout?

Tell the story

1

2

3

4

What time does this park open?
OPEN
CLOSE
AM
PM

What time does this park close?
OPEN CLOSE
AM PM

Suggestions for extending the use of this **talkabout** book . . .

The page headings are only brief suggestion as to how the illustrations may be used. However, these illustrations have been planned to help children understand various important concepts during their discussions with you. For example, you can talk about the children in the first 'playground' picture going **up** and **down** on the see-saw, **dowr** the slide, and **round and round** on the roundabout. You can also talk about the various human actions to be seen in other pictures—running, climbing, sitting, bending-over, picking-up, mowing, planting out, sweeping, etc.

In many of the illustrations (particularly, for example, the 'Look and find another like this' and 'Match the pictures with the black shapes') visual differences of shape and colour can be pointed out. The ability to